Everyday CALM

A **52-WEEK** Inspiration and
Mindfulness Journal to **RESET**,
REFRESH, and **LIVE BETTER**

Published by Sourcebooks
P.O. Box 4410, Naperville, Illinois 60567-4410
(630) 961-3900
sourcebooks.com

Printed and bound in the United States of America.
VP 10 9 8 7 6 5 4 3 2 1

Introduction

. . . .

Deep breath in.

The turmoil of the world and our day-to-day lives can often spill into our inner balance. Through burnout, stress, and exhaustion, it can be hard to build healthy routines that help you unlock inner peace and a daily sense of intention.

This journal was created as an escape of sorts—an opportunity to create those moments of intention throughout your week. By using this journal, you create time for yourself each week to hold time for peace, to hold time for goal setting, to hold time for nothing but thoughts of your own well-being; you create a mindset of calm that can center your week and your well-being. So close your eyes. Imagine a calming space. Take a deep breath. Turn the page and begin your journey.

Find Your Balance

· · · · · · · · · · · · · · · · · · · ·

Finding balance involves focus and practice, much like walking on a balance beam. Take a step back and consider areas of your life as if you were juggling them. What are the most important things you need to keep a hold on versus others that could drop once in a while? Acknowledge that there is give-and-take with most things in life, and you never need to "do it all." Living a balanced life is about being aware of your own strengths, recognizing how you spend your time, establishing healthy routines and boundaries, and staying in the present.

What is throwing your routine off balance? How can you course-correct?

Find Your Balance

Find Your Value

· ·

Finding our own value can be a big, big ask. Despite how it feels, despite how we often define it for ourselves...value is not measured by productivity or output. Value is not measured by what you create, what you do for others, or how much you deliver in your day-to-day life. As people, each one of us has inherent value. You as an individual, you have value simply by being. No matter how pulled you feel to produce, or how much you feel you need to do for others, this week try to keep in mind that you also need to serve *yourself*. Understand that you are your most precious mission in life, and creating anything beyond the best version of you is a secondary need.

How can you put yourself first this week? What value can you seek from yourself beyond productivity?

Find Your Value

Everyday Calm

Find Your Center

· ·

Finding your center, what drives you—the goal that all other goals, wants, and needs stem from—is a challenge. Take a moment now to slow down, close your eyes, and breathe. Think about what drives you. Is it your family or other connections? Is it success—creative or financial? Is it simply joy—your own or the spreading of it? By accessing what we want most, we can unlock our next paths forward by simply asking *Will this bring me closer to my biggest goals?* before we take next steps.

Center yourself in your goals and passions. Where do you want to be, and how can you align your inner desires to your experience?

Everyday Calm

Find Your Breath

. . . .

Finding your breath is a deceptively simple task, one to which many may pay no attention. Listening to your body and tuning into your breathing rhythms can greatly reduce stress levels. Are you pursing your lips? Sucking in your diaphragm? Taking shallow, rapid breaths? Be mindful of the quality of your breaths. Take slower, longer breaths deep within your stomach. More deliberate breathing will relax your nervous system and calm your disquieting thoughts and sensations. This practice of diaphragmatic breathing can feel strange at first, but with practice and compassion for yourself, you may find yourself more often in a state of calm.

When do you find your emotions most erratic or heightened? How can you build breathing into your routine and avoid such reactions?

Find Your Breath

Everyday Calm

Find Beauty

. . . .

Finding beauty can be nearly impossible when we are rushing from moment to moment. Take a second to slow down today and live in the present moment, savoring the beauty all around you. Find joy in the simple pleasures. The laughter of loved ones, the sunlight coming through the window. If you can spare the time and the weather allows, slip outside and breathe in the fresh air—take in the world around you. Step out of your standard routine to create a moment that is built to simply enjoy the world and those around you.

How can you break free from your routine centered around rush and savor something beautiful this week? Record what you noticed here when you slowed down and savored.

Find Beauty

Everyday Calm

Find Beauty

Find Security

Finding security can be both literal and spiritual. Take a moment to think about the people or things that make you feel safe, secure, or heard when you're stressed. What do they all have in common? Once you have tapped into what environments make you feel secure in yourself and make you feel heard and comfortable, try to figure out how you can replicate that feeling in all facets of your life. If there are people you don't feel secure around, how can you remove them from your routine and build a new routine around people you feel safe with? Recognizing that your own sense of calm and your own sense of security can be strengthened by the world around you offers you the opportunity to build a world where you feel confident and at peace day in and day out.

Where do you feel insecure in your day-to-day life? Is that emotion tied to a particular situation or individual? How can you flip the script?

Find Security

Everyday Calm

Find Security

Find Your Passion

. . . .

Finding your passion can bring joy and purpose to your life. We often place expectations and value judgments on our interests and what we think they should be. This fixed mindset can block you from discovering new passions and learning new things about yourself. Be open to new experiences, get excited about possibility, and find what ignites your interest. How do you like to spend your free time? What's holding you back from pursuing what gives your life meaning? It takes work to get out of your comfort zone and ignore perceived expectations. Let yourself be a beginner, try something new, and find time for what you love!

What excites you? How can you bring that excitement into your routine and make some big goals to move toward it?

Find Your Passion

Everyday Calm

Find Acceptance

· ·

Finding acceptance is not the act of resigning ourselves to who we are. Acceptance should be an act of jubilation, one in which you are accepting yourself flaws and all in an act of love. Much as we fall in love with others in our life and accept them for who they are with compassion and joy, we should love and accept ourselves. As Robert Holden said, "No amount of self-improvement can make up for any lack of self-acceptance." No matter how we try to change ourselves in the name of self-improvement, if we are working to change who we are through a place of shame and not a place of love, we will never find joy.

Have you truly accepted yourself? If so, what was the hardest thing to accept? If not, what's holding you back?

Find Acceptance

Everyday Calm

Find Acceptance

Find Support

· ·

Finding and building a network of support requires an act of vulnerability on our part. Take a moment and think about the last time you were overwhelmed. Now reframe that moment as an opportunity when you could have reached out to a loved one for help. When our feelings are too much, when the world feels like it is too much, often one of the best solutions we can pursue is reaching out to someone we trust. The support of our loved ones can make accepting our feelings a little bit easier and the path forward a tiny bit clearer.

Who is your biggest source of support? What special role do they fulfill in your life?

Find Support

Everyday Calm

Find Support

Find Wellness

. . . .

Finding wellness in your everyday life begins with acknowledgment and enrichment of core aspects of your health and well-being: emotional, spiritual, intellectual, physical, environmental, financial, occupational, and social. Take some time to think about what areas of your life are feeling nourished and tended to versus those that may need more attention. Are you feeling success financially in your job but lacking deeper connections with family and friends? Are you thriving at school and learning all you can but ignoring regular meals and hygienic routines? There is no singular path to wellness. Wellness starts with you and your awareness of what you want and need out of life.

What does wellness mean to you? What gaps do you see in your life compared to your definition?

Find Wellness

Everyday Calm

Find Stress Relief

· ·

Finding relief to our stress is not a simple trick. What works one day may not necessarily work the next. Therefore, it is important to be open to finding tools beyond ourselves for when stress is running high. Don't be afraid of seeking healthy, external resources to manage your stress! This journal is a great first step, but what other tools are in your arsenal? Perhaps an app for meditation or breathing? Have you explored in-person or online communities to build up your support structures? Looking beyond yourself for solutions to your internal stress doesn't mean you've failed, it means you're open to realizing when you may need more support.

What brings you joy in life? What brings you peace? What tools do you have to bring more of those moments into your routine?

Find Stress Relief

Find Transformation

· ·

Finding transformation means letting go of who we are now for the idea of who we might be. Moments of transformation are always tumultuous—the opposite of the calm we all seek. However, once we are on the other side of such change, we forget the struggle that led us there. As Maya Angelou said, "We delight in the beauty of the butterfly but rarely admit the changes it has gone through to achieve that beauty."

What change are you experiencing right now? How can you let go of the strife related to the process so you can transform into your butterfly?

Find Transformation

Everyday Calm

Find Peace

. . . .

Finding peace is about finding contentment within yourself and being okay with who you are, where you are in life, and what you have. Life is not a race nor is it a competition; sometimes we can get lost in the pressure to always keep moving, always keep winning, and always keep striving for the next thing. Often, it is less common for people to take a break and stop occasionally to appreciate all they have achieved in life. Being at ease with yourself and finding contentment in the simple things can lead to peace of mind, a healthier lifestyle, and even self-fulfillment.

List ten simple pleasures that give you contentment. How can you build at least half of them into your schedule this week?

Find Peace

Everyday Calm

Find Your Goals

. . . .

Finding our goals is often a process that asks us to ask more of the world. You deserve all the happiness the world has to offer, so what makes you happy? How can you create long-lasting happiness? Knowing your biggest goals, what actions will help you get there? Close your eyes and clear your mind. Imagine you've achieved your biggest goal. How are you feeling? What steps led you there? Slow down and work your way backward, unpacking each small moment that will lead you to this dream...and then open your eyes ready to begin with those first small steps.

Write down some of your goals for the week. Don't worry if you don't achieve all of them. It's a way of centering yourself for the next few days, not a contract that must be fulfilled.

Find Your Goals

Everyday Calm

Find Your Goals

Find Grace

Finding grace requires us to give ourselves room to make mistakes and for others in our life to have such room as well. Often, one of the most efficient paths to inner calm is working through the anger and resentment we have for others that is always on a simmer in our consciousness, ready to pique to a boil at any moment we call it forward. By holding onto our grudges or annoyance, we are holding onto turmoil. Particularly in instances when the person our anger is centered on is completely oblivious, this is an exercise in creating stress for the sake of stress.

What negative feelings are your harboring that you need to let go of? How can you do so?

Find Grace

Everyday Calm

Find Grace

Find Your Joy

. . . .

Finding joy is often found in the small moments, like sitting outside in the warm sun, eating freshly baked cookies, seeing an old friend, or relishing in a good night's rest. Joy is a spark—it can be a fleeting surge of positivity but, if you nurture the flame, can grow into a greater state of delight and satisfaction with your every day. Start looking for the meaningful things in life, both big and small. Make room for your passions, dreams, and goals. Cultivate a mindset of growth and inspiration. Seek laughter, light, and positivity. By being true to yourself and your needs, you can always find new reasons for happiness.

Plan out a path to build more happiness into your routine. List five simple actions below that will better support joy in your day-to-day.

Find Your Joy

Everyday Calm

Find Your Pulse

· · · · · · · · · · · · · · · · · · · ·

This week we're quite literally asking you to take a moment and find your pulse. Sit with your feet flat to the floor, close your eyes, and place a hand on your heart. Feel the rhythm of your heartbeat against your palm. Breathe deeply. Slow down. Breathe deeply a few more times. Do you feel your heart rate slowing down? Take a few minutes to sit in peace with the feel of your own internal rhythm.

How did you feel connecting with your heart and body?

_____

_____

_____

_____

_____

_____

_____

_____

_____

Find Your Pulse

Everyday Calm

Find...Nothing

· ·

When were you last asked to find nothing? Do nothing? Take a moment and allow that moment to not hold anything in particular and produce nothing with it. Find a cozy spot, perhaps a sunny corner, perhaps somewhere quiet, and settle into it. Take a moment to stare into the distance for a time, doing nothing whatsoever for five minutes.

How do you feel when you intentionally do nothing? How do you feel afterward when you make the time to have space for yourself that isn't asking anything of you?

Find...Nothing

Find Your Reset

. . . .

Finding your reset is something you have the power to do when you're feeling stagnant or unhappy with your current situation. Reflect on your position as a whole and analyze where you need to make a change. It can be helpful to accept where you are, and recognize that—while you cannot change the past—you can change the future. Let go of anything that is holding you back: declutter your home, say goodbye to people who are bringing you down, and relinquish any negative feelings that are preventing your fresh start. Remember, resetting your life does not have to happen overnight and often takes place over a series of smaller, attainable goals.

What do you need to let go of in order to reset?

Find Your Reset

Find Friendship

· ·

Finding friendship isn't asking you to make a new friend but rather maintain and celebrate the friends you already have. Check in with a friend or close family member today. Maintaining relationships can be difficult, especially in times of turmoil or stress, but they're important for our overall mental health. Friends and the feeling of comradery can help us bring a calm to the storm, as both a sense of comfort and voice of support.

After you checked in with your friend, how did you feel? What can you do moving forward to replicate the positive results that came from connecting?

Find Friendship

Everyday Calm

Find Friendship

Find Your Yes

. . . .

What's something you'd normally find difficult that you can say yes to today? When we are rushing through our standard week, it is often all too easy to say no to new experiences that come up. Take some time today or this week to intentionally make room for *yes*. See what might come from it.

What did you say yes to that you would normally have said no to? What happened and how did you feel?

Everyday Calm

Find Perspective

· ·

Finding a new perspective on things can start as easily as envisioning an old lesson from childhood: put yourself in someone else's shoes. Taking time to step outside of yourself and view the world through a different lens can be eye-opening and lead to new developments in self-discovery and empathy. Changing your mindset for the better by opening yourself up to new experiences, reducing any negative self-talk, and pulling yourself out of ruts can do wonders for your viewpoint on life. Being more intentional about the way you think and the choices you make is a helpful way to begin altering your worldview.

Think about a recent problem you've been trying to solve. What alternative perspectives might exist? If there are others involved, what can you see from their perspective? Perhaps flipping the scope can help you resolve things!

Find Perspective

Everyday Calm

Find Perspective

Find Intention

. . . .

Finding intention doesn't need to be a Herculean effort. All it takes to be intentional is to focus and *slow down*. Instead of eating dinner in front of the latest streaming show, put on some soft music with your meal that will give you space for conversation or room to think freely. Instead of watering your plants in the morning while making your mental to-do list for the day, talk to your plants while you water them. Notice how they are looking, how they are absorbing the water. Find small moments where you can make more space for intentional living instead of going through the motions.

After trying to make more space for intention this week, what did you notice in your world? What delighted you?

Everyday Calm

Find Intention

Find Presence

· ·

Much like intention, find presence this week and explore the space you take up in your interactions with others. Explore your interactions and consider who you were in each moment. Do you like who you are putting forward? Do you feel present with others and with the world? Take a moment and try to be present within it. Press your feet into the ground beneath you. Enjoy the sensation of the world pushing back up against you, reminding you that you are present in this moment.

How much of your week did you feel present for? Why or why not?

Everyday Calm

Find Presence

Find Kindness

. . . .

Finding kindness begins with being kind, not only to others, but to yourself. Be honest with yourself: are you always as compassionate toward yourself as you can be? Think of yourself as a friend or loved one, and ask yourself how you might treat them and show them care. Being kind to yourself can cultivate a lifestyle of kindness. Pay someone a compliment or let them know you appreciate them. Hold the door open for someone, do someone a favor, or even just give them a smile. Kindness is contagious; it can make you and others feel good. You might be surprised by how many people appreciate everyday kindness!

How can you spread kindness this week? Make a plan and record the results here.

Find Kindness

Everyday Calm

Find Awe

Find awe in your every day. One easy pathway to awe is through art. Find a piece of art in your city that you love. It can be a mural, a poster, anything. If you can't physically visit a piece of art, pull it up virtually and pore over it. Why do you love it? What makes it special? Use the art as a lens to connect with yourself today and experience awe.

What art did you take in? What about it struck awe in you?

Everyday Calm

Find Motivation

· ·

Take some time this week to find motivation for something you've been putting off. What is something you've been avoiding facing or completing? Take some energy from your other tasks and focus on tackling this one. It's been draining your energy and without it looming over you, who knows what you can achieve next.

How did it feel unleashing yourself on your dreaded task? How can you prevent yourself from delaying next time something you don't want to do comes up?

Find Motivation

Find Gratitude

· ·

Finding gratitude can start with the little things in life—nothing is so small that you can't appreciate it. A warm, sunny day in the middle of February or receiving kind words from a colleague can be momentous occasions for recognition and appreciation. The trick is to be intentional and to practice being mindful about what happens to you. Take a few moments daily to actively think about several things you are grateful for and acknowledge that feeling in your body. Practicing regular gratitude can literally alter brain patterns and promote a healthier, happier, and more empathetic lifestyle.

How can you practice regular gratitude? List three things you're grateful for now.

Find Gratitude

Everyday Calm

Find Gratitude

Find Warmth

. . . .

Fill yourself with warm, comforting vibes this week. First by thinking warm, sunny thoughts about a task you were dreading...and then by literally bringing warmth into your physical space. Make yourself a hot drink, and as you take that first sip, allow yourself to relax. Pay attention to the way the drink warms you from the inside and imagine that warmth is thawing out some of your road blocks to inner peace.

What positive thoughts helped you look at the world with a warmer, sunnier outlook this week?

_____

_____

_____

_____

_____

_____

_____

_____

Find Warmth

Everyday Calm

Find Warmth

Find Your Space

. . . .

Find and make space for yourself this week. Take some time to make sure your environment is one of peace. If making your entire home Zen feels too daunting, start with one small area for yourself and take time to make it calming and comfortable. Somewhere you can both think serenely and accomplish goals. A clean space calms the mind.

Once you made space for your own peace and Zen, did you notice it was easier to create a state of calm? Describe your space and how it serves you.

Find Your Space

Everyday Calm

Find Your Space

Find Strength

· ·

Finding inner strength can support you through tough times. Sometimes, it's easy to lose sight of yourself in the face of struggles and become discouraged or hopeless. Remember to remain grounded and confident in yourself. You are your own person, and you have control over how you react and respond. Your struggles do not define you—in fact, they can sometimes be blessings in disguise. Being laid off from work can free you to pursue your passions. A breakup may help you realize you deserve the right person. Be honest with yourself to cultivate your strength. But remember, reaching out to others when you need support is only another sign of strength.

When was a time in your life where you had to tap into your own strength? How could that inner strength serve you in your normal routine?

Find Strength

Everyday Calm

Find Strength

Find Movement

....

Find movement and add it into your routine this week. If you can make the time, move your body fully by doing an activity such as taking a walk or doing yoga. Notice how your body flows through the motions, and focus on how you feel with each movement. On a smaller scale, simply do something with your hands and take note of how it feels to do something different. Write with a pen and paper. Draw. Practice shuffling cards. Focus on just the movement of your fingers.

How did you decide to put more movement into your week? What did you notice?

_____

_____

_____

_____

_____

_____

_____

Find Movement

Everyday Calm

Find Movement

Find Quiet

. . . .

Find a moment for quiet today. No music, no TV—just you and the silence. Breathe the peace in through your nose. Exhale the stress out through your mouth.

By turning off and tuning out all distractions, what did you gain from your moment of quiet?

_____

_____

_____

_____

_____

_____

_____

_____

_____

_____

_____

_____

_____

Everyday Calm

Find Quiet

Find Bravery

• •

Finding bravery doesn't mean you're never afraid! Quite the opposite. Bravery begins with admitting vulnerability and acknowledging the fears and insecurities you carry with you. Instead of viewing fear as a weakness, consider it an opportunity to practice courage. To grow your bravery, you will need to step outside your comfort zone. But never fear, bravery comes in many forms: standing up for yourself, defending what you believe in, supporting a friend, or even standing down and knowing when to compromise. Perseverance alone is a form of bravery: if at first you don't succeed, don't be afraid to try, try again. After all, tomorrow is a new day.

How were you brave this week? How do you feel now?

Find Bravery

Find Happiness

Finding happiness is often easier said than done, but let this be a gentle reminder to you that happiness is found not in the outside world but from within. Disconnect your definition of happiness from external forces, and focus on making your own happiness. What does internal happiness look like to you?

What are some small things that make you happy? Could you incorporate a few into your week?

Find Your Pride

. . . .

Find your pride—in yourself, in your work, in who you are, and in all you are accomplishing. It's easy to be proud of our loved ones, of those around us we see as high achievers, and to think of ourselves as average or even low achievers in comparison. Take some time this week to focus on your own skills, your own amazing feats. Focus in on what you give the world and how much better off it is for having you in it.

What is something you're proud of accomplishing? Remind yourself of your successes, and look to some recent wins.

Find Your Pride

Everyday Calm

Find Your Pride

Find Your Focus

· ·

Finding focus in a demanding world is easier said than done. To sharpen your focus, make sure you are eating a balanced diet, getting enough sleep, and exercising regularly. Then, assess your environment. Is your workspace too loud or cluttered? Try to minimize distractions like muting your phone or turning off the TV. Instead of multitasking, set a timer to give your full attention to single tasks one by one, then take regular breaks. Finally, practice your mindfulness, and try to be more present in every moment. Don't think of the past or worry about the future. Focus on the now.

How can you create focus in your day? In your week? What moments do you find yourself fully present and focused on?

Everyday Calm

Find Your Dreams

Find a path forward to your dreams. The first step is simply believing you can make them happen. Take time to jot down some goals and dreams in detail and a few rough steps to get there. Everything seems more attainable once it is written down.

List two of your biggest dreams and the few first steps you can take to achieve them.

Find Your Dreams

Everyday Calm

Find Your Dreams

Find Mindfulness

· ·

Finding mindfulness often starts with how we begin our day. Find one morning task you can do mindfully: making your bed, brewing your coffee. Use that time to connect with your body and your mind before the day ahead. Make sure that whatever you do, you're taking time to connect to your surroundings. Engage all your senses in living.

What can you add to your morning to create a moment of mindfulness? Did you see any difference doing so this week?

Find Mindfulness

Find Mindfulness

Find Connection

. . . .

Finding connection in an age of instant global communication and social media is, ironically, perhaps more difficult than it has ever been before. Everything is in the palm of your hands, so why do you sometimes feel isolated? What are the kinds of connections you would like to forge with others? Deep friendships? Long-lasting or meaningful communities? Take time to consider what you value most in relationships and pursue those things. Forming strong bonds and a feeling of closeness can improve our overall physical and mental health, assist with emotion regulation, and strengthen empathy.

What does lasting connection look like to you?

Find Connection

Everyday Calm

Find Connection

Find Energy

· ·

Finding energy when the world or you yourself feel tumultuous is easier said than done. The key to energy is realizing what's blocking it and how to rekindle it within you and your routine. If you feel burned out, try writing out what you're experiencing. What thoughts or feelings are the most overwhelming right now? Can you spend time on something less stressful for a while?

What roadblocks exist between you and the energy you need this week?

Find Energy

Everyday Calm

Find Energy

Find Forgiveness

Find a way to forgive yourself for the mistakes you have made or may make soon. It is often easier to forgive others than for us to forgive ourselves. Take the time now to give yourself some grace—an opportunity to learn and grow. Forgive yourself for mistakes you might make. It's important to grow, but it doesn't help to be mean to yourself while you do.

What is something you haven't forgiven yourself for? How can you move forward?

Find Forgiveness

Find Forgiveness

Find Trust

. . . .

Finding trust in both yourself and others starts with growing the belief that you are someone worthy of trust. Begin with self-compassion; change your inner thinking that sends you spiraling into self-doubt and self-criticism, and shift into a pattern of support. Ask yourself what you need to get through something or what it might take for you to have faith in yourself. Embrace your vulnerability and be authentic. If you can trust yourself to do whatever is best for you, in time, you can build trust in others. Building trust in relationships can take time, and you are the only one who can set the pace that is right for you.

How can you trust yourself more and be kinder to yourself? What language do you need to hear and tell yourself?

Find Trust

Everyday Calm

Find & Reflect

. . . .

Take some time revising your year so far. We're almost to the end of your fifty-two weeks, or one year, of calm. Spend some time reflecting on the best moments of your calming journey this week. It's easier to remember the things that frustrated us, but it's more valuable to remember the things that brought us peace.

Which exercises so far have you found the most impactful? What lessons have you carried forward?

_____

_____

_____

_____

_____

_____

_____

_____

_____

_____

Find & Reflect

Everyday Calm

Find & Reflect

Find Nature

. . . .

Find and get lost in nature this week. Nature is the great rejuvenator. Make some outdoor plans this week and reach out to friends to enjoy them with you. As Khalil Gibran said, "Forget not that the earth delights to feel your bare feet and the winds long to play with your hair."

How did your excursion into nature go? What did you feel, notice, and experience?

_____

_____

_____

_____

_____

_____

_____

_____

_____

_____

_____

Find Nature

Find Your Boundaries

· ·

Finding and setting healthy boundaries is a process that can take time but will help your physical and emotional well-being. Boundaries can help empower you to make your own decisions and to take responsibility of your own life. Create and maintain the boundaries that are right for you, whether that's asking someone for more space or telling your boss you can't work late at night. Trust in yourself to decide what's right for you, and don't be afraid to lean on a support system. Clear boundaries will help enhance your self-esteem, protect yourself, and foster healthier, mutually trusting relationships.

What boundaries did you build, or saw you need to build, this week?

Find Your Boundaries

Everyday Calm

Find Your Boundaries

Find Gentleness

. . . .

Find gentleness this week by taking a time to unpack your own vulnerabilities. Allow yourself to be fragile and explore. Be as gentle with yourself as you are with others. You deserve the same respect you give to everyone you encounter.

What emotions are hard for you to face? How can you help build these up from a place of gentleness and not shame?

Find Gentleness

Everyday Calm

Find Guidance

· ·

Find guidance this week, be it from a mentor, friend, or partner. Asking for guidance is not a show of incompetence. It's a sign that you are driven to succeed. By having someone confirming your direction and guiding you forward in your goals, you have a built-in system of support. You're allowing someone to take the energy off of you alone and share in your journey to growth.

What guidance did you seek out this week? How did it serve you?

Everyday Calm

Find Guidance

Find Your Inspiration

· ·

Finding inspiration can sometimes feel impossible when you're facing a creative block or lack of direction. Start by changing your environment—change rooms, go outside, travel somewhere—it's amazing how a simple change of scenery can spark a new way of looking at things. Spending time in nature, reading a good book, journaling, or listening to new music are other ways that are sure to snap you out of a funk and set you on a path to nurturing different parts of your mind. There is no one way to find inspiration, but sometimes the best way to find it is when you're not trying.

What inspired you this week?

Everyday Calm

Find Your Inspiration

Find Your Momentum

· ·

Finding and maintaining momentum is perhaps the hardest part in any journey. Watch something move today—a river flowing, the cars on a street, some trees in the wind. Breathe with the same steady motion you see. As your fifty-two weeks of calm come to a close, start to consider how you'll continue moving forward each week and building calm into your routine.

How do you find the motivation to keep moving forward? What inspires you to hold steady and allow room to grow?

Find Compassion

Finding compassion for ourselves is far, far more difficult than finding it for others. What are some times you know you put too much pressure on yourself? Answer honestly. It's okay to have high expectations for yourself, as long as you also have understanding and compassion.

Exploring the specific example that came to mind, how can you find more compassion for yourself? What triggers do you recognize that you'll need to combat?

Find Compassion

Find Your Calm

. . . .

Find *your* calm. What does calm mean to you? Close your eyes and picture a scene of relaxation. Where is it? What does it look like? Stay there for as long as you need, and let the calm wash over you.

How can you create relaxation like the scene you envisioned this week? How can you move forward into your next chapter with calm in the center of your routine?

Find Your Calm

Everyday Calm

Conclusion

....

...And exhale.

As you come out of this calming journey, our hope is that you have felt the impact that intention and calming moments can have on your week. As you plan for what's ahead, make sure to give yourself grace and support. You are, after all, your biggest source of support and peace.

Give yourself today, take a moment and relish in it. Your life is only beginning—there is always more to come.

Notes

Notes

Everyday Calm

Notes

Everyday Calm

Notes

Everyday Calm

Notes

Notes